www.finishinglinepress.com

QUOTIDIAN

poems by

Caroline Holme

Finishing Line Press
Georgetown, Kentucky

QUOTIDIAN

ACKNOWLEDGMENTS

Publisher: Leah Maines

Editor: Christen Kincaid

Cover Art: John Holme

Author Photo: John Holme

Cover Design: Elizabeth Maines McCleavy

Printed in the USA on acid-free paper.
Order online: www.finishinglinepress.com
              also available on amazon.com

Author inquiries and mail orders:
Finishing Line Press
P. O. Box 1626
Georgetown, Kentucky 40324
U. S. A.

Table of Contents

Shut-In

The grass is burning while the air hangs
thick with sweat. I stay inside, not much cooler,
in suspended animation, idling
restlessly, caught in the undertow
of day. Weeds take a deeper hold
on the patio. A fly buzzes round
the room. Some days are carrion, when I'm
merciless, pecking at futile dreams
I can't release. Without warning
my life turns one-dimensional again—
a chronic loneliness near evening—
I'm finding my way back to a place
where I never felt at home,
as if I could repair the damage done.

Message in a Bottle
for my mother

You pine, growing thinner,
a long way from home.

I pill my aged cats with steroids
and painkillers,

nagged by my own spells of illness,
dreading to fall and not get up.

End of childhood, as you cut me
down to size, call it as you see it:

you've outlived your God,
and I can't get out of my own way.

Through a rainy windshield,
I see the end in everything,

out past the beach at low tide—
its stony places I dread to cross—

into the drag of waves crawling
up the sand.

Sorrow takes my sandcastle like the sea.

April Elegy

Sharp sparks of snow like Indian flints on the wind strike my face and carve me up. My father's birthday rolls around. A taut, gray-white April sky promises showy weather, the day ahead of me, on the cusp of morning.

One year after his death, I remember my father here on earth, as if I could call him on the phone. Small—human size—and a little weird.

The blizzard stops, replaced by sun. I marvel at April in Connecticut, keep thinking of my father, who could never get enough. He read aloud, cried as he read. Responded to Rembrandt by painting. Kick-ass intense. Never even wanting to be selfless. Given to sneering.

We sat outside at 2 o'clock one summer morning, sleepless, facing the moon in the night sky. Everything pointing to the darkness— Look!—where art comes from.

Here, tiny darts of rain on the wind. You could call the sky gray.But nothing stays.

Then sun again.
Then threatening.
Then snow.

The Widow

She picked a headstone
for punctuation
though the grave yet yawned
like nausea.

She shook, pushed on—
a tedium
of leftover hours
pressed the point home:

the red, red rusted
tin roof of the shed
raw under gray-
lidded cloud—

where she heard the cold
clang of the gate shutting—
shutting out,
shutting in—

as the heart hung
from its hinges,
too heavy to open,
trapped her within.

Undergrowth clammy
at summer's end
with shining traces of snails
journeying the rose leaves...

Second Skin

The year I got sick:
aqua, this robe—awful.
My father drove.
I picked it out.
He charged it to Lord & Taylor.

My nightie was terminally
ripped. I feared
it would fall away
with my father in the house
exposing me to the chill draft
(I dreamt I ran naked to school).

I needed a cover-up,
knotted the belt tight
hugged my knees up close.

Our story begged to be told
but no one was talking.
We were alike: I hated us.

He nailed me, deep dark blue
lily I was, glowing
in the April evening
like a flare on the highway
(steer clear).

Years later
the robe is stained with coffee
stiff with spills
and decay, vandalized
by a hole at the nape
where it hangs
on the hook in my closet.

Skin

I'm like a snake
struggling to grow out
of my skin, itching in the grass
rubbing past rocks
shrugging free—
and I bite.

Betrayal

1.

After recess we settled down
into our classroom—
  small birds to roost—

Miss Mason read us a long, slow poem
like a lullaby—
and we were hushed,

gazing at the unknowable
names carved in our desks
of children gone.

2.

In my pocket I held a note
from my best friend
I saved to open

alone in my room after school.
It revealed how I
was hated, like a snake's fang.

the room spun—
flooded with shame—
I told no one.

3.

Next day I sweat in the heat
of an early spring.
Miss Mason flung

the windows wide. The steaming
radiators still
pumped as if it were winter.

I had to shoot
my hand up first,
bully the boys on the bus.

Kick stones down
dead-end streets
for fun.

Drunk

Discovered by her father
making out with a boy on the couch,
stereo cranked up loud, door shut.

Coming out of a blackout, dumped by her date
on the front steps, blood pouring from the chin
from a fall, too drunk to stand up.

Naked—except a shower cap—
she raced across the street
in front of cars, to entertain her friends

Hospital at Night

From the eighth floor
the city is a checkerboard
of trees rusted with winter.
White squares border houses
where snow has caught—
and steeples reach—
avenues of headlights stretching north
onto the sleepless highway—

I'm restless for morning
while the T.V. buzzes
high in the corner of my room,
the words of Jesus
counterpointed
by ads for perfect abs.

Waiting is everything here.

With a shower and a clean jonny
tears come—
salt then sweet then salt—
melting the hard nub of anger
in my chest—
starburst.

You Felt the Cold

Still, indefatigable in love.

A woolen skullcap hugged
the gentle moon of your face
warm in the frigid evening.

Finally, they found
the tumor strangling you.

As you lay
in the mechanical bed
I said a prayer;
you cried;
I held onto your hand;
you kept slipping away.

******

Now the telephone
cries out: grief calls
every day, like a friend;
but when I pick up
no one is there.

All things echo your voice.

Stay

I gag at wakes.
Estranged by death, I cannot match
my feelings to the fact.
There is a hollow where my heart should be.

Something about Paula
made me want to linger,
love her more
abandoning her to oblivion—
the dark January ocean—

Standing on the beach
with shoes of ice
in a ferocious wind
watching her ashes go—
I wanted to say
Stay, Paula—
stay.

Sunday's Child

Shock rolls through the first day without you.
Rain speaks of a long, bleak future.
Sunday, gutted of light.
I'm left with the hollow afternoon.

Rain speaking of loss:
You got in past my guard, now you're gone.
I reel from the walls of the afternoon.
How did I come to rely on you so?

You got past my guard. Now you're gone.
Going nowhere, irrelevant,
With no link to the world,
Demons people the hollow.

I'm irrelevant, rudderless, when pain
Bursts into Sunday gutted of love;
Demons people the hollow;
Shock rolls through the first day alone.

Commuter Train

There never was a handsome
pin-striped guy
who turned his head toward me
with a melting eye;

admitted me to privileges
of shiny hardwood
floors, three-car garage—
suburban ease;

stepped me up
into identity
with cosmetic, polished nail
and ash-blond dye.

Anonymous, I run
the clean-cut gauntlet
of indifference—
walk home alone.

Weather

"And the rain it raineth every day..."
(Twelfth Night)

The pleasure of weather is this:
I like the mystery and change:
I don't pretend indifference
to the blind eye of the inscrutable sphinx
ready to pounce in a snowstorm
or such: like an animal grabbing me
in its paws: hot—hot to the extreme
then raw: not insulated from
its claws, but awed by the naked majesty of
the kaleidoscope sky—silver lining
and storm's eye—with me abroad
in it, out on the road in all of it,
wandering through weather
and pondering why—

Broken Silences

I square off
against the cat litter box
morning and evening

locked in for this minute,
submit, dutiful, day after day,
silence broken by distraction—

pay taxes, keep house,
show up for work, comply
with the price of a few friendships,

maintain my attitude with lists
of things to be grateful for,
and walk the bases ball after ball

thrown by an inept pitcher, or
perform my life like an audition,
acting as if I could love like anyone else—

while I long to be snowed in,
casting out
for the ken beyond my ken—

when you cancel at the last minute
or step out of the checkout line
to chase a forgotten item, while I wait,

or go on too long in my meeting
my heart swells like a bloodblister
greedy, pushy, cheating.

I give my cat 4 or 5 cruel jerks
as if she were a stubborn saltshaker,
throw her to the floor—

Spring Fever

Skunk cabbage whispers acrid
to the sharp air; the brook rushes
in tongues, unfurling mud.
Treetops shudder and the cuckoo
echoes down wooded halls.

I rediscover you as the ducks return
to their old neighborhood, fluffing
their pinfeathers, diving for weeds, bobbing
on the pond rough with whitecaps. They know
better than to birth their ducklings
before there is warmth and food.

So I demur, putting you off.
One moment I love you, the next
regret it; weather uncertain,
cloud and sun racing above—hurry—
wait, no—
come

Quotidian

I look up from my work at eleven
and drag on my coat to go out,
joining the smokers to try on the cold.
It's gray. I don't feel like working.

I drag on my coat and go out—
any length to escape from my desk.
I feel grim and I don't want to work.
Monday I'm glad to have someplace to go,

but soon I'll do anything for a break,
even if just to check the clock.
Monday I'm glad to have someplace to go,
but Tuesday's a desperate prayer.

Even the act of checking the clock—
work draws me in like a drug, I forget.
By Tuesday I'm desperately praying.
In toil I'm relieved of my private affairs.

Work numbs me like a drug—not to think!
Daydream of a holiday casts a mirage;
in toil I'm relieved of my private affairs,
while I long for escape—that too like morphine.

Daydreams of holidays cast a mirage.
I follow a buddy outside in silence
long for escape—that too like morphine.
We look to the sky for the weather.

I follow a buddy outside in silence—
a flock of birds swirls up from the street.
As we look to the sky for the weather,
tiny explosions of energy soaring,

birds in the wake of a car in the street
catch me off guard for a moment;
these tiny explosions of energy soar—
birds—lift me on winter wind.

Caught off-guard in the moment
out with the smokers to try the cold
birds lift me into the winter wind
released from my work at eleven.

Northern White Violets

The full moon, huge, looks down
like a cepacol lozenge that soothes
the wild, harsh, sore yearning in my throat.
It's faith I'm after, faith in what is
whole and shared.

Winner take all. Once, as a child, losing
a birthday party game, I split off,
dark descending early. The will
to win like a boomerang cut me down.
It's faith I'm after—even small, even
in solitude. I had to face the devil
across the kitchen table with our contract
between us, up for renewal. We argued
back and forth like lovers: I defiant,
twisting words every which way, shouting
to make my point. He, obstinate
with his hope-killing smile. I faced him
at the table under the fluorescent glare.
He reached out and snatched my future from me—
I hung on and fought—the pages started to
tear—I let go
destitute

The scene melted to white violets
clustered in a worn corner in the grass.
White violets looking up, reflecting
the moon in their pale faces.

Purple Tulips

Tulips never really open.
They come to the house
crisply shut, aloof, imposing,
petals folded over a profound blue chasm,
desiring only to be ignored.

Each pursues its destiny
isolated from the rest
except by the tacit knowing
that they are now the last—
cut from their bed,
counted by a strange hand
to end up here
in a glass pitcher.

Tulips never really open, except to die.
You have to guess
the quiet, serious development
of their folded thought
from the sarabande of their decay:

Petals turn darker
and darker purple every day—
so many shades of blood
toward black—
tips curl minutely backward.
Petals twist and unfurl

fling out an arm—broken—
and broken, totally surrender:
splayed, exposing a white
throat.

The Birds Are Back

Heralding from borders south
making a green racket in the underbrush
come robin, cardinal, unhoused.
My hearing though is jaundiced
with the last of snow on which they write
the jingles that find their counterpart
in inner ear—their complex
polyphonies, precursors of Bach's
sobrieties on the pianoforte—
guessing more icy rain
of a lingering winter.

Dread still dominates.
A bird upstages my alarm at 4 a.m.—
the mournful, persistent call
to prayer, joined by one and then
another, and again—distant. Still
I doubt, forget how to hope
but listen like the deaf—longing only—
for the ken within my ken;
make them a place in my redbreast
of silence, of patient
preparation for their song.

Caroline Holme received an American Academy of Poets and a Ruth Lily prize at Smith College. Finishing Line Press published her first chapbook collection, COLD CRUMBLING, in 2012. She studies at the Hudson Valley Writers' Center in Westchester, New York with Jennifer Franklin, Fred Marchant, and Alex Dimitrov.